D0829100

Marco Pierini

PIENZA

Guide to the town and surroundings
Corsignano, Spedaletto,
Monticchiello, Sant'Anna in Camprena

Foreword by Bruno Santi

nuova immagine

Photographs:

Fabio Lensini, Siena: pp. 16, 18, 20, 21, 22, 23, 26, 27, 28, 31, 32, 33, 34, 35, 36, 37, 41, 45, 46, 55, 56

Bruno Bruchi, Siena: pp. 9, 10, 11, 12, 13, 14, 15, 24, 39, 40, 43, 44, 47, 48, 49, 50, 52, 53, 54

ISBN 88-7145-136-8

via San Quirico 13
I-53100 Siena
Tel. 0577-42.625 – Fax 0577-44.633
e-mail: nie@biemmepro.it

First published, April 1999
Second edition, March 2002

Translation: Miriam Grottanelli de Santi and Lisa Grottanelli de Santi
Revisione: Teresa Davis, Venetia West

Photolithography: FIM, Siena
Printed by: Centrooffset - Siena
Cover: Pienza, the Cathedral (photograph: Bruno Bruchi, Siena)

INDEX

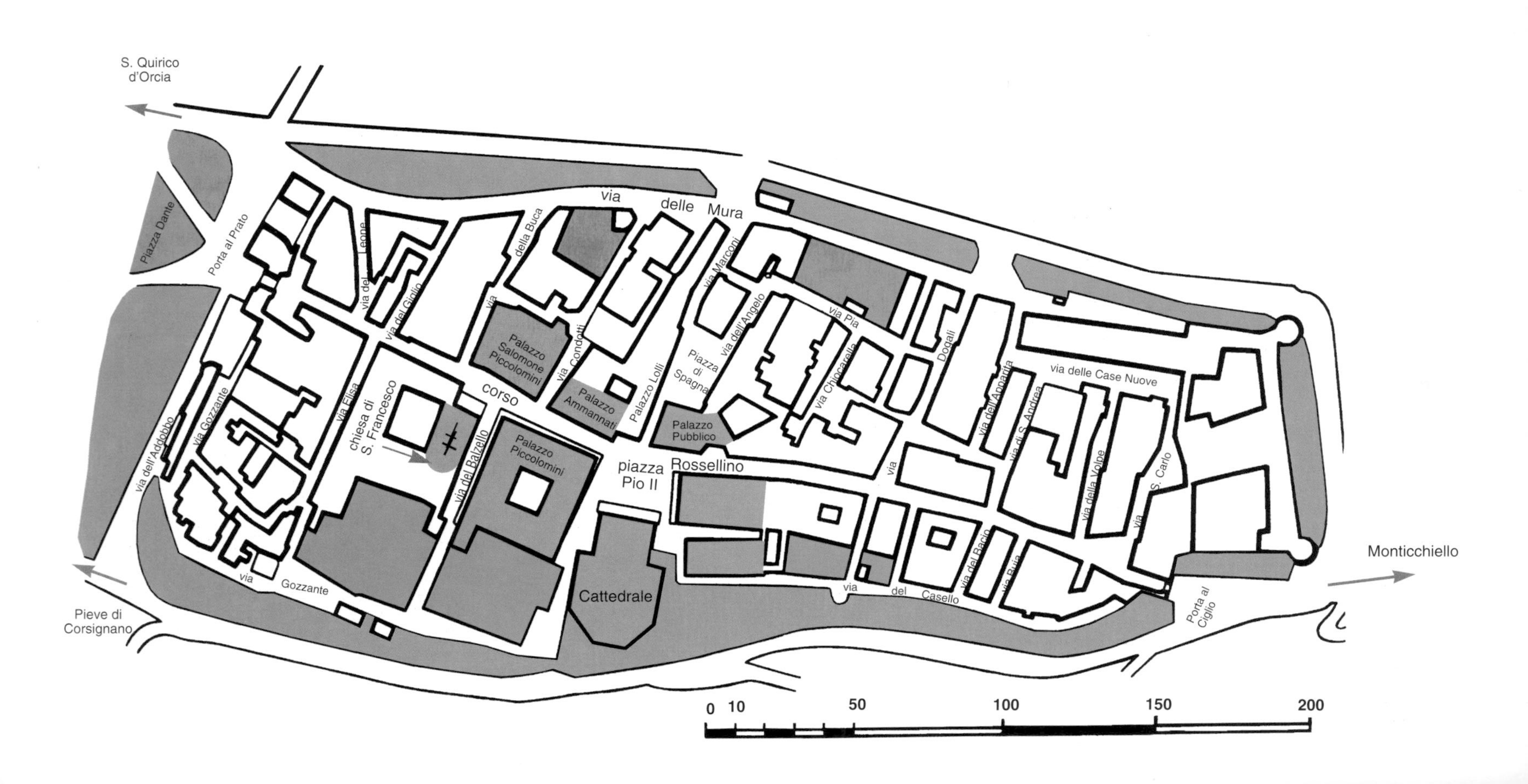

S. Quirico d'Orcia
Piazza Dante
Porta al Prato
via delle Mura
via del Leone
via del Giglio
via della Buca
via
Palazzo Salomone Piccolomini
via Condotti
Palazzo Ammannati
Palazzo Lolli
via Marconi
via dell'Angelo
Piazza di Spagna
via Pia
via Chiocarella
Dogali
via dell'Apparita
via delle Case Nuove
via di S. Andrea
via della Volpe
via S. Carlo
Palazzo Pubblico
piazza Pio II
Rossellino
corso
chiesa di S. Francesco
via del Balzello
Palazzo Piccolomini
via Elisa
via Gozzante
via dell'Addobbo
via Gozzante
Cattedrale
via del Casello
via del Bacio
via Buia
via
Porta al Ciglio
Monticchiello
Pieve di Corsignano
0 10 50 100 150 200

FOREWORD

Recently Pienza has undoubtedly been amongst the most visited and appreciated centres around Siena. It has thus overturned its century old tradition of a solitary city, the peculiar expression of a humanistic dream never fully realized, still admirably complete in itself, in its fantastic geographic location, in a dominant position overlooking the hills of the Val d'Orcia and enclosed by the majestic curtain of the Monte Amiata.

The extremely delicate urban texture of Pius II's city is certainly running many risks because of mass tourism. One of these is that it loses its natural features. Pienza is taking on that exterior look that the metropolitan tourist expects a "marginal" community to have retained. Shops sprout up from what appears to be an ever more rarefied and specialized productive base. There are too many antiquarian and herbalist shops for a city that lived off the products of an agricultural and pastoral hinterland. Crowds gather full of curiosity around products that can only be called pientine in that they are sold in Pienza.

Thus the image of the city is a distorted one; and yet one should not forget that the constant flow of visitors has checked the inevitable degradation that Pienza would otherwise have suffered through the abandonment of its inhabitants. The local administration with great foresight has not allowed modern buildings to interfere with the old town. It is not by chance that UNESCO has declared this city in the Val d'Orcia to be one of their protected centres, together with a number of other prestigious towns. Pienza has thus been rightfully acknowledged for its artistic heritage bound to one of the most interesting and important figures of the Italian Renaissance.

And yet it is not easy to speak about Pienza: it's tempting and up to a point even justifiable to simply celebrate its architectural and artistic beauty; it is dangerous to let oneself be too attracted by a variegated tradition that validates everything and takes everything for granted. One can lose oneself in front of rhetoric and not understand the subtle meaning of the Pientine creation, the essence of wisdom and art, a figurative culture that has been able to combine Florentine form with Sienese spirit producing an unrepeatable work of art and that we can truly appreciate through the words of someone who really knows this city.

This is in fact the case of Marco Pierini, a young scholar who has not been overcome by the scientific rigor of the Università degli Studi in Siena and whose work has always shown his passion for the visual aspect of art similarly to his teacher, the indefatigable Enzo Carli, Soprintendente, art historian, researcher, whose bibliography proves his dedication to the history of Siena and of Pienza.

Marco Pierini's work is rich in information and observation that really help us to better understand and appreciate what we see. And even though his book is very informative it is never pedantic because he very cleverly adds a personal touch to the information.

We are sure that Marco Pierini's contribution to the rich bibliography that has grown around this beautiful little Tuscan town will soon earn a reputation for its unmistakable quality.

Bruno Santi
Superintendent of Artistic and Historical Assets
of Siena and Grosseto

PIENZA

Panorama of Pienza

HISTORICAL NOTES

It was during his stay there in February 1459 that Pope Pius II made his resolution to build a new church and a palace at Corsignano, the village where he had been born with the name Enea Silvio Piccolomini fifty-four years before, and which was in the brief space of three years to become "Pius' town", even in its name: Pienza[1].

The place which was destined to become Pienza has a very long history of settlement. The excavations undertaken around the parish church of St. Vito and St. Modesto, which is just outside the built-up area of the town – in an area rich in water supply and of favourable climate – have proven an unbroken line of settlement from the Neolithic period up to the Middle Ages. The study of the local place-names makes it clear that there was a Roman presence, starting with Rutiliano (the first name under which the territory of the church is recorded), down to Corsignano, the name which is met starting from the year 828 and which falls into disuse only with the foundation of Pienza[2]. The village, with the passing of time, moved from the parish church to the little hill above, where a church was built dedicated to the Madonna. In 1932, in the course of the restoration work on the cathedral, the foundations and

The town walls along Via del Casello

fragments of the sculptural decoration were discovered – and then the basilica and convent of San Francesco, the only Medieval monument as such which survives in Pienza.

Enea Silvio Piccolomini[3] was born in Corsignano, where his family owned considerable property, on the 18th October 1405, and he spent his childhood there before moving to Siena and starting studies in his beloved humanism and in jurisprudence (which he loved less).

At the age of twenty-eight he left to follow Bishop Capranica in the direction of the Council of Basle, thus starting on his highly acclaimed political and diplomatic career and at the same time his ecclesiastic studies.

We can follow the most important events in his life as illustrated in the wonderful frescoes by Pinturicchio (1505-07) on the walls of the Piccolomini Library in the Duomo in Siena: the ambassadorship to the King of Scotland; his coronation as poet by the Emperor Frederick III (1442); the submission to Pope Eugenius IV (1445) – after he had been secretary to the Antipope Felix V; his nomination to become Cardinal; his election to the papacy (1458); the Congress in Mantua which he summoned in the attempt to persuade the princes of Christendom to undertake a new crusade (1459); the canonisation of St. Catherine (1461) and, finally, the arrival in Ancona, where he had wanted again to try to organise a new crusade against the Turks, but where he instead met his own death (1464).

Piazza Pio II

A fine humanist and a lover and promoter of the arts, Enea Silvio Piccolomini has left us a rich collection of writings in Latin, which covers a wide range of subjects and genres: from the Plautine comedy *Chrisis* to the unfinished *Cosmographia,* and from a love story (the celebrated *Historia de duobus amantibus*) to what is his most famous work, the *Commentarii,* an autobiography in the form of a diary of the years of his pontificate, a valuable source also for the reconstruction of the events relating to the building works in Pienza.

The architect to whom Pius turned was the Florentine Bernardo Gambarelli, known as "Rossellino", a pupil and collaborator of Leon Battista Alberti, but there is no doubt that the prime mover of the whole stet was the Pope himself, who would have discussed his ideas not only with Rossellino, but also with Alberti, as is documented by Pius II on the occasion of the journey to Mantua in 1459 [4]. Pienza, according to an Albertian precept, adapts itself to the pre-existing Corsignano and does not disturb the layout of its streets: the piazza with its new modern buildings is placed at an angle to the Corso and the latter, although embellished with the palazzi built by the Cardinals – on the specific orders of the pope – has not modified its course nor lost its irregularity. The Piazza does not have one privileged, frontal approach, but side-entrances permitting different kinds of views in. Seen in perspective, facing the front elevation of the

The "Well of the Dogs" in Piazza Pio II

Duomo, the piazza seems to slope back steeply; there is no appearance of depth but instead a pre-eminence of the Cathedral which seems to step forward from the countryside of the Val d'Orcia in the background, as if to cut the space short. Looking the other way, with one's back to the Duomo, the piazza seems to be aligned in an exaggerated perspective and appears deeper and larger than it is in reality. The equilibrium and the perfect calibration of the relationships between the buildings is also emphasised by the division of the paving in the piazza, laid in a design of large rectangles. In addition, the fine well (known as "The Well of the Dogs"),

located almost on the corner of Palazzo Piccolomini, is based on a drawing of Rossellino, as is confirmed by the range of Renaissance decorative motifs employed and the grace of its insertion into the piazza.

The Cathedral

THE CATHEDRAL

The Cathedral rises up on the site of the ancient parish church of Santa Maria, but is orientated in a different direction. The earlier church in fact had its façade looking onto Palazzo Piccolomini and the apse pointing towards Palazzo dei Priori (where Palazzo Borgia now stands), with its main entrance in the side which adjoined the piazza. The new church was intended to go up with its façade looking over the piazza and was built with its presbytery extending out over a

The bell-tower and apse of the Cathedral

precipitous slope of tufa and clay, which became unstable even before building work was finished. Since the beginning of the 16th century restoration and consolidation work on the Cathedral has been necessary because of the collapse of the zone around the apse; the visitor can see by simply walking down to the presbytery the massive difference in levels[5].

The church in this alignment however responded perfectly to the scenographic requirements for the piazza, setting itself up as an architectural backdrop placed against the vast panorama of the Val d'Orcia and Monte Amiata (the apse could be seen from a great distance away in the valley) and, furthermore, thanks to its massive windows, it acquired an extraordinary luminosity, at every time of day and in every season. The importance of light and its mystical and aesthetic function in the interior of the Cathedral is well documented in many parts of the *Commentarii,* as well as in the definition which Pius II himself gives of the Church as *domus vitrea*[6].

The travertine façade, with its simple shed structure, is subdivided by four great pilasters into three parts which correspond to the nave and aisles of the interior, and are decorated by massive arches bearing on columns which clearly show Alberti's influence. Inside these are the three entrances into the church and, above, two very classical niches and an oculus in the centre. The pediment is divided by two elegant candelabra (bas relief decorations on pilasters) and has

The Cathedral interior

a garland in the centre circled around the papal coat of arms. Carli has rightly supposed that the sculptural works on the façade – definitely designed by Rossellino – were carried out by Sienese master craftsmen[7].

The external walls and the apse of the church are built in sandstone and have beautiful windows, of an elegant gothic

Cathedral, Sano di Pietro, Virgin and Child enthroned with St. Mary Magdalene, St. Philip, St. James and St. Anne

design. The slim, graceful bell-tower rises up on the left (looking at the façade); the upper part was rebuilt, in all probability as a faithful reconstruction of the original design, after the earthquake of 1545.

The bell, cast by the Sienese founder Giovanni Tofani in 1463, who recast the old one from the church of Santa Maria, bears an inscription by Pius II[8].

The interior, on a Latin cross plan, is divided into a nave and two aisles – all of the same height, following the model of the *Hallenkirchen* which Pius II had learnt to appreciate in his sojourns in northern Europe – separated by two rows of piers with attached half-columns, with elegantly decorated capitals and tall dosserets painted with false marbling. Two of the half-columns, the ones which flank the entrance to the bell-tower, make allusions (according to Pieper, who confidently identifies Alberti's hand in the project) to the two builders of the Duomo: one in fact represents a crayfish ("gambero"), an obvious reference to Gambarelli, the surname of Rossellino, and the other a mask among foliage which is meant to be a portrait of Leon Battista Alberti[9]. There are five chapels in the cathedral, each one lit by a huge window: two form the arms of the transepts and three more open off the apse.

Pius II was tenacious in his desire to heighten the effect of the light and he did not want any illustrated or coloured glass, nor did he want – again following a precept dear to Alberti – any painting on the walls to disturb the whiteness of the surfaces, and so for the decoration of the interior he commissioned five altarpieces by four Sienese artists: Lorenzo di Pietro (known as "Vecchietta"), Sano di Pietro, Giovanni di Paolo and Matteo di Giovanni, who made two[10].

The paintings, all datable to before the 29th of August 1462 (the day of the solemn consecration of the Cathedral), with the exception of the panel by Giovanni di Paolo dated 1463, respond to the aesthetic stipulations laid down by the new architectural style of the Duomo: they are bare of the very ornate woodcarving of the gothic style, with its cusps and pinnacles, and even of the predella, with its illustrated stories, and they are no longer divided into compartments but have their figures disposed together in the same space, enclosed within an architectural frame and surmounted by a pediment or by a figured lunette.

All of them have three little "tondi" at their base: in the altarpiece by Sano di Pietro, the centre scene displays *St. John the Baptist* while the side pieces make up a scene of the *Annunciation*; in the second altarpiece by Matteo di Giovanni, the *Crucifixion of Christ* is displayed in the centre between two Saint figures; in the third altarpiece, the central "tondo" shows *Christ in Pietà* enveloped by a *Grieving Madonna* to its left and *St. John the Evangelist* to its right; on either sides the Piccolomini coat-of-arms.

The first painting we come across, on the wall to the left is the one which Matteo di Giovanni executed lastly, maybe already after the death of Pius II. It displays the *Virgin and*

Cathedral, Lorenzo di Pietro, known as "Vecchietta", The Assumption of the Virgin with St. Agatha, St. Pius, St. Callistus and St. Catherine of Siena

Child Enthroned between Saints Girolamo, Augustine, Nicholas, and Martin and manifests a complete understanding of the Renaissance space, particularly evidenced in the depth of the marble throne.

Following, in the first chapel is the *Virgin and Child enthroned with St. Mary Magdalene, St. Philip, St. James, and St. Anne* by Sano di Pietro. The artist, an illustrious, if rather repetitive, representative of the Sienese tradition, by now in his mature period, complies only in exterior form to the revolutionary spirit advocated by Pius II. His altarpiece, coloured preciously and expertly made, is anchored in the old styles of gothic, it completely lacks depth and even the unity of space is only apparent, because the saints, as Carli has written, "appear still isolated, as if they were still enclosed within the narrow outlines of the compartments of a polyptych"[11].

The altarpiece in the next chapel represents *The Assumption of the Virgin with St. Agatha, St. Pius, St. Callistus and St. Catherine of Siena* and is considered by many to be the masterpiece of Vecchietta, a painter and sculptor of central importance in Siena in this period. The tripartite division which separates the main scene from the pairs of saints, which distinguishes this painting from its three companion pieces, should not be interpreted as a return to the past, but is dictated essentially by iconographic reasons and brilliantly resolved with its highly original architectural structure, of classical origin, as a gable, or rather, a "façade". The spatial and compositional qualities of this work are notable also in the invention of the backgrounds for the saints: bold glimpses of interiors with coffered ceilings.

Extreme care has been taken in the execution of the painting and appears in the minute exactitude of the details of garments and jewellery; in the engraving, polishing and etching of the gold to draw out all luminous effects possible, and in the subtlety with which the landscape is portrayed[12]. Below the open sepulchre of the Virgin is the artist's signature, which at first seems rather strange: "OPUS LAURENTII PETRI SCULTORIS DE SENIS", but is not in fact so extraordinary, because many of Vecchietta's sculptures carry the signature: "OPUS LAURENTII PETRI PICTORIS..."[13].

Pius II had to turn to Sienese craftsmen again for the beautiful wooden choir-stalls, very finely carved and inlaid, in the central chapel of the apse. They are still very gothic – just as the columns and huge windows of the church are gothic – with windows with two lights in a pointed arch, multi-foiled and divided by slender twisted columns, and rosettes which all have different decorative motifs. On the bishop's throne, at the top, the Piccolomini coat-of-arms is carved, while the date of execution, 1462 (in Roman numerals), can be read on the cornice which runs along the top of the stalls. The great lectern in the choir on the other hand, is in fully Renaissance and 'Florentine' style; constructed at the same time as the stalls but probably according to the design of a more modern artist.

The third chapel of the apse contains an altar made of travertine, surmounted by a ciborium the design of which can be surely attributed to the hand of Rossellino. The altar table is

Cathedral, the choir-stalls

clearly a recent replacement, whereas the ciborium, with its architectural structure closely related to the frames of the altarpiece paintings, with the taste and expert choice of its decorative motifs taken from ancient models, and with its exquisite craftsmanship, make this tabernacle an object of sustained quality. It used to contain a sacred gift which Tommaso Paleologo made to Pius II in 1462: a reliquary bust in gold and silver containing fragments of the skull of St. Andrew. Pius II had a new reliquary bust made in 1463 for the display of the relics in St. Peter's by the Florentine goldsmith Simone di Giovanni Ghini, who was working in Rome as goldsmith to the papacy. When the relics and the reliquary were given back to the

Cathedral, the tabernacle

metropolitan bishop of Patras by Paul VI in 1964, he sent Ghini's precious reliquary – which today can be found in the Diocesan Museum – back to Pienza in exchange[14].

The Virgin and Child with St. Catherine of Alexandria, St. Matthew, St. Bartholomew and St. Lucy by Matteo di Giovanni, the youngest of Pius II's four painters, bears witness to a ready application to the new Renaissance style further confirmed as we have seen in the altarpiece executed for the same Cathedral a few years later: it features the perspectival convergence of the floor, a plausible disposition of the figures in space and, above all, the lunette with the *Flagellation* which recalls as if in quotation the vigorous drawing style of Pollaiolo.

The last altarpiece, on the right wall next to the door of the sacresty, is by Giovanni di Paolo: in this the Virgin and Child

Cathedral, Matteo di Giovanni, Virgin and Child with St. Catherine of Alexandria, St. Matthew, St. Bartnolomew and St. Lucy

are surrounded by angels and by St. Bernardino, St. Anthony the Abbot, St. Francis and St. Sabina. By this stage Giovanni di Paolo was more than sixty years old and he, like Sano di Pietro, finds insurmountable difficulties in adapting himself to the new style. He tries to resolve the unity of space by concentrating the saints' gaze onto the Child, but all it takes is for St. Sabina to turn her eyes elsewhere for us to notice her separation from the context of the painting; the bodies of the figures do not occupy the space (irrationally defined by the floor plane inclined against perspective), but seem almost to stick onto the surface, as if they were silhouettes

cut out and glued on. His distance from the Renaissance aesthetic and themes did not however prevent Giovanni di Paolo from creating one of his masterpieces, especially in the lunette, with its very touching *Pietà*, a dramatic image of Mary and the angels watching over the broken limbs of Christ in a strange, almost lunar scenery, made up only of rocks and little hills, which seems to allude to the landscape of the nearby Crete.

Cathedral, Giovanni di Paolo, Virgin and Child surrounded by angels and by St. Bernardino, St. Antony the Abbot, St. Francis and St. Sabina

Painting on the walls, as we have said, has only a marginal presence in the interior of the Cathedral of Pienza, being

Palazzo Pubblico and, on the right, Palazzo Borgia in Piazza Pio II

limited to the two *Angels carrying the papal emblem,* painted by a collaborator of Vecchietta in a fresco on the great arch which stands above the choir and in the decoration of the vaults (restored in modern times following the traces which have emerged from underneath the plasterwork [15]).

CHURCH OF SAN GIOVANNI

The church, built under the apse of the Cathedral, is reached by a little door at the base of the bell-tower. There is a fine baptismal font designed by Rossellino and made in travertine in his workshops, decorated with typical motifs from Renaissance art to which he added, in honour of his client, the Piccolomini crescent.

Built into one of the walls are the remains of the sculptural decoration from the ancient parish church of Santa Maria, which came to light in 1932 following the restoration of the Duomo; amongst the fragments of cornices, capitals and mouldings something stands out which must have been the lintel of the doorway to the church, with scenes carved in bas relief of stories from the Old Testament.

DIOCESAN MUSEUM

On the top floor of the Palazzo Vescovile is the Diocesan Museum in Pienza [16] *(open 15 March to 31 October: 10-13 and 14-18, closed on Tuesdays; 1 November to 14 March: 10-13 and 15-18, Saturdays and Sundays only)*. Opened in 1998, the Museum is fully furnished with heart of the rich collection once held in the Museum of the Cathedral. The

Palazzo Vescovile is made up of two buildings: the Palazzo Borgia which looks onto the Piazza, and the Palazzo of the Cardinal, Francesco Jouffroy of Arras, which overlooks the Corso Rossellino. The Palazzo Borgia stands to the left of the Duomo and opposite Palazzo Piccolomini, on the site where, in Old Corsignano, Palazzo Pretorio stood. The remains of this building were perhaps partly plundered for the erection of the residence of the powerful and dissolute Cardinal Rodriguez Borgia, who was later to become a most famous pope under the name of Alexander VI and father of the equally renowned Caesar "Valentine" and Lucrezia. He donated the Palazzo in 1468 to the Episcopate, who still maintains it to this day.

The façade is very simple but of elegant Renaissance taste with string-courses above which are aligned windows in the form of Guelph crosses and a fine internal courtyard with a well in its centre that can be accessed from the Museum.

In the **first room** there is the *Crucifix* from San Pietro in Villore dated at the end of the 12th century which is one of the pictorials found in the area around Siena. Another is the early 14th century *Crucifix* from the church of San Francesco from the school of Duccio, which is now attributed to Segna di Bonaventura, after the personality of the "Master of San Polo in Rosso" – to whom the crucifix was previously ascribed – merged into that of Segna[17].

Also in San Francesco there used to hang the painting of the *Virgin and Child* the centrepiece of a polyptych now dismantled, believed to be the work of Bartolomeo Bulgarini and datable between the 1340s and 1350s. The *Madonna with Child* by Pietro Lorenzetti, originating from the church of Monticchiello and temporarily being kept in the Diocesan Museum is of exceptional quality. It is one of Lorenzetti's more stimulating paintings in which the sweet glances of mutual understanding between mother and son are magnificently represented.

Last to be mentioned, with a polyptych that was once in the church of San Lorenzo in Monterongriffoli which is attributed to the school of Ugolino di Nerio, three small paintings by Niccolò di Segna, part of a dismantled triptych, and finally, a late 13th century precious illuminated *mass book* by an anonymous painter in the style of the Umbrian and Sienese schools,

Museum, Lorenzo di Pietro, known as "Il Vecchietta", Virgin and Child enthroned with St. Blaise, St. John the Baptist, St. Nicholas and St. Florian

to which two illuminated initials were added by Lippo Vanni during the second half of the 14th century [18].

In the **next room**, there is a small *pyx* of the second half of the 13th century that comes from a workshop in Limoges. The *pyx*, circular in shape, is made of gilt copper and is decorated with enamels with rather stylised plant motifs. Another *pyx* in gilt copper by a Sienese goldsmith dates from the second quarter of the 14th century: it has a sturdy and very gothic architectural structure and a knob decorated with six "champlevé" enamels with elegant figures of birds and dragons [19]. Another object worthy of mention is the *chalice* by the Sienese goldsmith, Tommaso di Vannino, dated in 1420 and comes from the parish church of San Lorenzo in Montefollonico.

The *reliquary cross* signed and dated in 1430 by the Sienese goldsmith Goro di Neroccio is of great value even though it has been modified over time and lacks certain parts.

A portable triptych originating from the church of Spedaletto in Val d'Orcia, which is datable to the second half of the 14th century is subdivided into forty-eight little *Scenes from the life of Christ.* This may be an illustration of a "religious epic poem," as Carli has suggested [20], or more generally a portable altarpiece evidently used for instructional purposes. The episodes represented are very popular and direct with open references to the stories on the back of the Maestà by Duccio; the unknown,

Museum, "Master of the Pietà", Scenes from the life of Christ

modest painter has been identified by Meiss[21] with the "Master of the Pietà", a Sienese artist from the early 14th century who takes his name from the considerable number of representations of this subject attributable to his hand.

The great altarpiece of the *Madonna della Misericordia* (the painting surface was transferred onto canvas at the end of the 19th century), is the work of Bartolo di Fredi, signed and dated 1364. It is the finest work of the artist's later paintings and brings to mind Simone Martini and the close link to the frescoes which Bartolo left on the left-hand wall of the collegiate church of San Gimignano in 1367. The faithful all have different expressions and characters. They are gathered on their knees under and protected by the cloak of the Madonna, whose hem is held up by two charming angels, and among them, Torriti has recognised the first figure on the left to be Emperor Charles IV who played a fundamental part in Sienese politics in the mid-1360s[22]. If this identification may justify the hypothesis that the altarpiece comes from a Sienese church, it

Museum, Ugolino di Nerio, Virgin and Child with St. Marcellinus, St. Laurence, St. Leonard and St. Augustine the Martyr

seems however that it cannot be referred to 1354 as Torriti suggested, thus disclaiming the careful reading that Brandi had already made of the badly deteriorated text in 1931 [23]. The son of Bartolo di Fredi, Andrea di Bartolo executed the *Virgin with Child* which comes from the convent of San Sigismondo in Montefollonico, painted sometime between the end of the 14th century and the beginning of the 15th century.

Very well preserved and of notable quality is a small portable triptych of the *Madonna of Humility*, surmounted by *God the Father blessing among Angels and Prophets* and flanked, on the side panels, by *St. John the Baptist* and *St. Elizabeth of Hungary*. On the pinnacles above we find *The Angel Gabriel and the Virgin Annunciate*. Datable to between the end of the 1430s and the early 1440s, this little triptych, once attributed to Sassetta, is today rightly inserted in the catalogue of the "Master of the Osservanza," that gifted Sienese painter who takes his lead straight from Sassetta and shows a close affinity with Sano di Pietro (so much so that Brandi proposes to identify him with the latter in his earlier period). The attribution to the "Master of the Osservanza" for our painting did not convince Carli however who preferred to create a new artistic personality, akin to Sassetta, who he called the "Master of Pienza" [24].

Beside that is a small portable triptych of the Maestà, and on the cusps of the hinged panels we find *The Angel and the Virgin Annunciate*, *The Adoration of the Shepherds* and *The*

Crucifixion. An old notice carries an improbable attribution to Giottino, while Carli thinks it is the work of an "artist from Siena or Umbria from the second half of the 14th century," Martini believes it is by an artist from the Florentine school[25].

Originating in the parish church of San Leonardo in Monticchiello, is a statue of *St. Leonard* in walnut, which is well preserved but has been completely repainted in this century. It is attributed to the Sienese sculptor Domenico di Niccolò "dei Cori" and dated to the years 1415-1425.

Another statue, again in walnut and with its polychromy for the most part original, is attributed to the same artist, but to his more later years (1430-1440). This represents *St. Regolo* and comes from the homonymous chapel in Palazzo Massaini. The bishop-saint, according to legend "master" of St. Cerbone, is represented – recalling his decapitation – in the unusual iconographical stance of a figure holding his own severed head in his hands[26].

Continuing we find three *northern european tapestries* of the highest quality and datable to around the mid-15th century. The oldest represents *The Crucifixion* and is claimed to be either of Arras or Tournai manufacture. The other two, perhaps manufactured in Brussels, illustrate *Jesus meets Jairus and heals the woman diseased with an issue of blood* and *The Articles of the Creed*. The three tapestries show many similarities to Flemish paintings from the same period and also reminiscent of the work of masters such as Roger van der Weyden[27].

Isolated in the **fourth room** of the Museum inside a glass showcase especially designed in 1901, we find the most valuable work: the *cope of Pius II*. Donated to Pius II by Tommaso Paleologo, according to tradition, it was then given by the pope to the Cathedral of Pienza. This splendid cope with twenty-seven *Stories from the life of the Virgin of St. Margaret of Antioch and of St. Catherine of Alexandria*, is of English manufacture, fashioned according to that most delicate and highly prized embroidery technique known as "opus anglicanum".

The vivacity of the narrative, the refinement of the figures and layout which is pure gothic in style, the minute description of naturalistic motifs and the masterful balance of colours make this work of embroidery a masterpiece of English art from the first half of the 14th century, and is considered worthy of the highest admiration even in surroundings like those of Enea

Silvio Piccolomini, which were steeped in Renaissance culture. It seems preferable to date it to around the first half of the 14th century; stylistic and chronological correspondences have inspired attempts to identify the designer of the drawings, transferred so wonderfully onto material by the craftsmen, with the anonymous illuminator of the *Holkham Bible* (London, British Museum) [28].

There are two paintings by Vecchietta in the Museum. The splendid *Virgin and Child enthroned with St. Blaise, St. John the Baptist, St. Nicholas and St. Florian,* which once hung above the main altar in the nearby church of San Niccolò in Spedaletto. The painting should be taken in the strictest connection, chronologically and stylistically, with the niche built for the Cathedral in Pienza: this too is in a frame (according to Renaissance precepts), it rejects subdivision into compartments and the woodcarving of gothic, and is structured as a single central piece surmounted by a lunette and supported at its base by a step with a figured predella. What is more, the church of Spedaletto – a farm belonging to the Hospital of Santa Maria della Scala in Siena, which also commissioned the painting, as is indicated by the two coats-of-arms placed at the edges of the step – was reconsecrated on the 4th of September 1462, not even a week after the consecration of Pienza, and it is very likely that by this date the altarpiece was already finished. The disposition of the figures in one open space, defined by a colonnade and by a wall of coloured marble, the luminosity and the harmonious chromatic range, and the evident wish to embrace perspective are all elements which Vecchietta acquired and brought to maturity under the guidance of contemporary Florentine painting, in particular the work of Domenico Veneziano [29].

An interesting fragment of predella recovered from Sant'Anna in Camprena, portraying the *The Death and Resurrection of the Monk*, representing the miracle of St. Benedict which was supposed to have occurred during the building of a convent. The attribution to Vecchietta, advanced in the 1930s by Mason Perkins and subsequently by Berenson, finds confirmation in more recent critical writing and the dating seems close to that of the altarpiece of Spedaletto [30].

The three display cases in this room, hold objects of notable interest. The so-called *Chasuble of Pius II* resulted from an

Museum, the cope of Pius II

assembly, maybe in the 17th century, of 15th century fabrics; the Saint figures on the each side of the garment are the work of a German or Flemish embroiderer. Beside the *chasuble* is the priceless *crosier of Pius II*, in embossed silver, engraved and decorated with enamel. The knob, shaped like a little Brunelleschian tempietto, and the *putti* who carry the Piccolomini family coat-of-arms suggest an object of Florentine culture, and in all probability it was given to the Cathedral on the occasion of the election of the first bishop of Pienza on the 29th of August 1462 [31]. On the scroll of the *crosier* is a decoration of plant forms on an enamel plaque and two minute sculptures, both of kneeling figures, who represent the *Angel and the Virgin Annunciate.*

Inside the glass case in this room are sixteen silver panels of translucent enamel, of which fourteen are sewn onto two modern mitres, one is unattached and one is mounted onto a chasuble-clasp. They come from one single mitre, perhaps donated to the Cathedral together with the crosier, and represent the *Virgin and Child, the Annunciation, God the Father, the Holy Spirit, the Four Evangelists and other saints.* The panels too suggest a Florentine influence, from the circle of Maso Finiguerra, and the name which has been cautiously put forward is that of Piero di Bartolomeo Sali, a documented collaborator of Pollaiolo in a work for a reliquary intended to hold relics donated by Pius II himself to the church of San Pancrazio in Florence [32].

Together with the mitre and the crosier, the episcopal insignia was completed by a bronze ring, lost today, which was probably quite similar to the one kept in the Civic

Museum, "Master of the Osservanza", Madonna of Humility

Museum in Siena with the name and coat-of-arms of Enea Silvio Piccolomini. Also among the liturgical trappings donated by Pius II to the Cathedral in Pienza is a fine *vessel for holy water*, a *censer*, and an *incense gondola* made by a Florentine silversmith, displayed in showcases along with other works in gold.

Another object worthy of mention on display here is a *chalice* made by a 15th century German silversmith, simple and elegant with an unusual shape; a very large cup, a straight stem and no knob and a silver paten with an architectural structure which Carli proposes, with some doubt, to be the work of the Sienese goldsmith Pietro d'Antonio, datable to the time of Pius II [33].

The *reliquary-cross of the Patriarch Saba*, in gold filigree, is on the other hand of certain oriental provenance and carries writings in Serbo-Croat and in Greek; for historical reasons it is supposed to have been made around 1375, a date which accords with the style of the object; however we know nothing about how it came to Pienza[34].

Moving on there is a *cross* by a German goldsmith from the 15th century and the *reliquary bust of St. Andrew* executed by the Florentine Simone di Giovanni Ghini between 1462-1463, which was donated, as already mentioned, by Paul VI in 1964.

The little altarpiece with the *Virgin and angels in adoration of the Child* – which was in San Francesco in the 19th century, but whose original location is unknown – is an early work of Bernardino Fungai, probably datable to around 1490; there are numerous examples of similar compositions, characterised above all by the unusual physiognomies of the figures – childlike, gentle looking and with heart-shaped mouths – and it has even been suggested that they have all used the same cartoon as a common model[35].

Museum, Domenico di Niccolo "dei Cori", St. Regolo

There are three very beautiful compartments of a predella with *Stories of St. Sebastian*, the early work (around 1470) of Neroccio di Bartolomeo, influenced not so much by his master Vecchietta, as by the painter and miniaturist Liberale da Verona, from whom he takes his elegant rhythms and subtle graphic style[36].

More modest but not lacking in grace, is the *Virgin with Child, St. Anthony the Abbot and St. Sebastian* by Guidoccio

Museum, Fra Bartolomeo, Rest on the Flight into Egypt

Cozzarelli, which portrays a pictorial surface rather faded due to a past restoration effort.

On the wall is the large panel with the *Madonna della Misericordia* surrounded by two angels and, at the sides, Saints Sebastian and Bernardino. This is probably the work of Luca Signorelli, with a great deal of participation on the part of his workshop. The better parts of this work are evident in the delicate faces of the Virgin and of the devotees kneeling before her, whose character the painter has well depicted [37].

The canvas of the *Rest on the Flight into Egypt*, which was recovered some years ago in the Palazzo Vescovile, has been recognised by Torriti as the work of Fra Bartolomeo from the early 16th century [38] even if it does not appear to have the same sustained quality.

We also find on the walls various figured silks of Tuscan manufacture (perhaps from Florence) from the 15th century: one of the *Annunciation*, from the middle of the century (very similar to the work of the Florentine painter Giovanni di Francesco), three fragments of *Angel cross-bearers* from the second half of the century and a most elegant *Virgin in adoration of the Child*[39].

Museum, detail of a panel on the mitre of Pius II

A collection of Sienese paintings are located in a **small room** where also a fine tondo with a frame of gilt papier maché with the *Holy Family and the young St. John the Baptist*, a painting from the second quarter of the 16th century and is attributed to Marco Bigio [40]; a painting by Bartolomeo Neroni also known as "Il Riccio" portraying the *Virgin with Child, St. John the Baptist and St. Catherine* and three heads of biers – the fourth one is missing – of unknown origin. The clear derivation from the late work of Sodoma has led to their attribution to one of his followers, who Bagnoli recently has wanted to recognise as Lorenzo Rustici, an artist of slight and, for the moment, rather uncertain output [41].

Worthy, particularly for the short stories illustrated on the side of the main scene, is the canvas by Arcangelo Salimbeni who portrays *St. Dominic and St. Catherine receiving the rosary*, dated 1580.

From the parish church of San Leonardo in Montefollonico come two masterpieces of 16th century Sienese sculpture, from around the mid 1530s, created by an outstanding sculptor of the school of Cozzarelli and Beccafumi. The author of these two noble, intense and elegant figures has been identified – hypothetically – as Carlo Andrea Galletti (Siena 1499-1539) [42].

Scroll of the crosier of Pius II

The choral books from the Cathedral were written and illuminated for Pius II between 1460-1462 even if, according to tradition which has not been confirmed, they were made for the Duomo in Orvieto and subsequently acquired for 800 ducats by Pius II, who then had them illuminated by Sienese artists. Eight books are

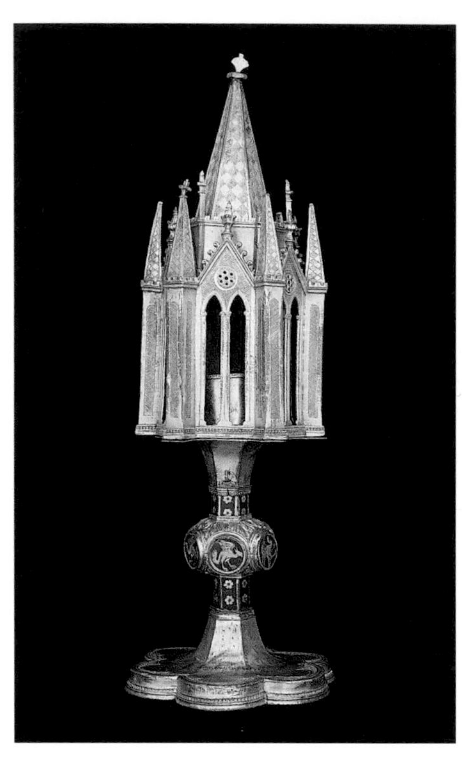

still held complete, but another five were damaged in 1904 and of the one hundred sixty-two illuminated plates that were stolen, only forty-nine have been recovered.

The corpus of the illumination of Pienza has yet to be studied in depth; at the moment scholars agree in attributing the psalm-book with the beautiful *Baptism of Christ* to Sano di Pietro (Antiphonary A.I.), three hymn-books to a Florentine illuminator (Antiphonaries A.III.-A.IV. and A.VI.) – who Carli suggests – presumptively – may be Fra Giacomo Torelli – and two books to the Sienese Pellegrino di Mariano, a prolific illuminator who particularly in these years reflects the influence of Sano di Pietro [43]. The remaining books (Antiphonary A.II. and Gradual G.II.) are attributed to two unknown, and rather modest, Sienese illuminators who were in the circles of Pellegrino di Mariano [44].

Museum, Sienese goldsmith of the second quarter of the 14th century, pyx in gilt copper *(above). detail (below)*

In the centre of the same room there is a large display-case which contains gold and other ecclesiastical articles. One very unusual object is the small cross carved in box wood and composed of some forty-four *Stories of Christ* portrayed in virtuoso style, animated by figures which seem to swarm over the cramped space. It is very difficult to date this object and place it within a cultural context, however, it was traditionally considered to be an object from 13th century Byzantium, whereas it is now believed to be from the 16th century [45].

There is also a very valuable *pyx-monstrance* in gilt brass made by a (possibly Sienese) silversmith between the 16th and 17th centuries. Removing the reliquary for the

Museum, tapestry of the workshop of Tournai, The Apotheosis of the Church Militant, Purging and Triumphant

Eucharistic display, the object could function as a pyx and, to this end, it fitted with a removable cup in gilt copper[46].

Also noteworthy is the small painted *cross* by the Florentine Niccolò Betti, from the end of the 16th century and the two tabernacle doors, also beautiful, painted with the figures of *St. Peter* and *St. Paul* by Bernardino Mei. On the wall of the room hang three of the five canvases made by Bernard Rantwyck towards the end of the 16th century portraying the *History of the reliquary of St. Andrew* (the other two arc in the next room). Four heads of biers by Niccolò Betti, the *Portrait of the Bishop Francesco Maria Piccolomini* dated around 1590 by Ventura Salimbeni and a sketch for the altarpiece of the Conservatory church, San Carlo Borromeo made by Francesco Rustici around 1620 are the more interesting pieces of the **next room**, whereas the last room, apart from a fine painting by Francesco Trevisani portraying the *Madonna of the Rosary*, is entirely dedicated to embroideries kept partly in a chest of drawers and partly in a showcase. Among the embroideries worth mentioning are a *chasuble* from the mid 15th century, a *cope* from the mid 16th century – accompanied by its *chasuble*, *stole*, and *mitre* – and a *green chasuble* from the early 17th century in embossed velvet with a geometric design of squares[47].

ARCHAEOLOGICAL COLLECTION

Near what was the old Cathedral Museum there is an interesting collection of archaeological material[48] from the countryside around Pienza and neighbouring areas, which today is awiating to be allocated to what will be the Archaeological Museum of the Commune.

The most outstanding group is constituted by the so-called Landi-Newton Collection, which passed to the Museum by donation in 1925. This collection was formed after a number of Etruscan tombs were found in the area around Borghetto in 1860. They contain mainly articles from the archaic period (6th century BC). The lack of any documentation of the situation in which they were found has not permitted anything to be reconstructed and the pieces are grouped typologically. Most numerous in the collection are the forms which are related to the ceremony of the symposium: goblets, *kantharoi, oinochoai,* amphoras and water-vases, almost all in bucchero, a clay found around Chiusi used for making vases, many with relief or cylinder decorations. These latter recall, in some cases, the scenes represented on the clay tiles of Murlo and of Acqua Rossa.

There are also vases of ceramic and of purified clay, some decorated with figures painted in red or black. The objects in bronze consist of libation-cups, drinking-cups, vases, strigils and little votive bronzes. Among the objects coming from other areas are a small *kilyx* from the Clusium Group and various funeral urns made of pietra fetida, almost all of them with inscriptions. After a theft at the beginning of the 1980s, the archaeological room was not opened again. All the material collected in it will go in the near future to form the Archaeological Museum of the Comune, in which it will find suitable exhibition space, together with the articles from the excavations and finds made in the last thirty years.

The material from the pre-historic settlement (from the Neolithic to the Bronze Age) will have a prominent position due to its importance, excavated in the area lying immediately below the passeggiata of Santa Caterina.

[Alberto Dondoli]

Palazzo Piccolomini

PALAZZO PICCOLOMINI

Pius II was involved first-hand in the planning of his own palazzo. Constructed of "pietra arenaria" and finished in travertine, it rises to the right of the Duomo, where the original Piccolomini houses were demolished for the occasion. The main façade faces the main street of Pienza. There is no doubt that Rossellino had Alberti in mind, particularly his Florentine Palazzo Rucellai, when he designed this building. In respect to Palazzo Rucellai, the Pienza building is much less rigorous, and for this is often underestimated in regards to its more famous model.

However, as underlined by Carli, the variants used by Rossellino (for example the smaller windows on the ground floor without frames and not aligned with the architrave of the door, and the paraste of the ground floor decorated in bugnato while those of the upper floors are left smooth), cannot be mistaken for Rossellino's errors of Rossellino, but should be

Palazzo Piccolomini, inner courtyard

seen rather as artifices for amplifying the horizontal lines in respect to the vertical lines, due to the subtle interlocking of lines and volumes which constitutes the sublime harmony of the piazza. A travertine bench encircles the walls of the palazzo, and eight windows on each floor open on the sides of the building, while the side which faces the Val d'Orcia is open in a beautiful loggia constructed in three architectural orders. The hanging gardens below, accessible by way of the elegant inner courtyard of the palace, once decorated in graffito, were one of the first examples of this kind in Europe.

When the direct descendance of the Piccolomini family was extinguished in 1962 the ownership of the palazzo went to the Società di Esecutori di Pie Disposizioni di Siena which has since opened it to the public *(summer hours: 10-12.30-16-19; winter hours: 10-12.30/15-18; closed Mondays)*. The visitability of the palazzo is limited to a part of the "noble" floor which is conserved intact with the furniture and paintings, a few that belonged to the Piccolomini family, and many others which have been acquired more recently by the same family.

From the entrance hall one arrives, to the right, in the dining room and to the left, in a salon tapestried in worked

Palazzo Piccolomini, Arms Room

leather, where, among other things, we find a *Portrait of Orazio Piccolomini* (died 1678). Passing through the first corridor, decorated with three *Allegories of the Seasons* (the *Winter* scene is missing) of the Florentine school of the 17th century, and a Florentine portrait from the end of the 16th century, one arrives at the grand Arms Room, so called for the impressive display of arms of every type and from every era (though some may not be authentic).

Among the pieces of furniture from various periods, the six *Battle Scenes* similar to those of Borgognone and the 17th

Palazzo Piccolomini, Pius II's bedroom

century *Portrait of a Man* in the manner of Justus Suttermans that hangs above the fireplace deserve attention. From here one has access to the loggiato which overlooks a splendid panorama. From the Arms Room one also has access to the bedroom of Pius II, furnished with a 17th century bed and with paintings of various schools and periods. In the arch of the doorway is a *fresco* from the first part of the 16th century with the portrait of Pius II.

Returning to the Arms Room one passes into a second corridor which leads to the vast space of the library. In completing the tour, one exits by crossing a third corridor in which there is a Venetian 18th century *portantina*.

PALAZZO PUBBLICO

This building was also requested by the Pope, and was built at the same time as the Bell Tower of the Duomo – perhaps based on a design by Rossellino – by Pier Paolo del Porrina and Puccio di Paolo. The Palazzo Pubblico frames the piazza on one side of the main street. The palazzo, which is the seat of the Communal Administration, also houses the Tourist Office, accessible by way of the loggia. The loggia with arches rising above robust columns with Ionic capitals makes up the ground floor. The upper floor presents four mullioned windows that look out onto the piazza.

The tower, built of brick, houses a clock that came from the Certosa di Pontignano to replace the original of which Pius II speaks in his *Commentarii*. Many commemorative stone plaques are built into the walls of the building, most of which are from the 19th and 20th centuries. Among these are two bronze medallions in bas relief accompanied by commemorative stones: one with the *Profile of Enea Silvio Piccolomini* realized, on the model of the *pontificate medallion of Pius II* created by Andrea Guazzalotti in 1460, by the Sienese sculptor Arnoldo Prunai in 1905 to mark the 500th anniversary of the birth of the pope, and the other, with the *Profile of Rossellino,* is the work of another sculptor from Siena, Bruno Buracchini, executed in 1965.

The Council Room, on the right-hand wall, displays a ruined fresco with *The Madonna and Child with Saints Ansano, Gregory, Matthew and Vito* (the guardians of the city), which was discovered beneath the plaster during the restorations of 1900. It is a work of mediocre quality, executed by a modest follower or collaborator of Vecchietta[49].

Towards Porta al Prato

The renewal of the city could not end with the invention of the stupendous piazza, but rather extended beyond to the rest of the residential area, especially in the present Corso Rossellino, which is the main street through what was ancient Corsignano, now Pienza, along which one finds the palazzi constructed by the Cardinals under order of the pope. Pius II had in fact imposed upon the Cardinals to contribute to the erection of the new city with one of their own palazzi. He also paid for the restoration of the façade of the palazzo of Salomone Piccolomini and had the Sienese architect Pier Paolo del Porrina build twelve new houses for the people in the area around the Porta al Ciglio, as is indicated by the toponym "Via delle Case Nuove", or Street of the New Houses.

All of this construction fervour, however, did not go on beyond the space of a few years. With the death of Pius II in August, 1464 – followed shortly thereafter by the death of Rossellino – the town lost all of its importance and of the prelates which had been forced to add to the project, only Cardinal Ammannati, enchanted by the pleasantness of the place and by its healthiness, continued to go there, but there was no further construction. Today it is very difficult to identify which structures are those of the Cardinals, except in the case of the more important palazzi.

Directly in front of the Palazzo Piccolomini, preceded by a smaller palazzo, which faces the piazza, identified by tradition as belonging to Gregorio Lolli, the nephew and secretary of Pius II is the palazzo of Cardinal Giacomo Ammannati, perhaps the pope's closest friend, and the person who gladly adhered to the pope's request. The façade of the palazzo, which still has two family crests, is decorated in graffito like most of the Pientine homes, though most of the plaster is in poor condition. This sober three-floor palazzo with guelf cross windows once had a loggiato,

Corso Rossellino

Church of San Francesco, façade

perhaps built a little later, but which has unfortunately been walled in. In any case, it has maintained its inner courtyard, though it has been heavily reworked. The next owners were the Newton family.

Beside the Palazzo Ammannati is another which belonged to Salamone, however, according to tradition it was believed that its residency had been taken up by the Cardinal Atrebatense (or, Francesco Jouffroy). It displays Gothic mullioned windows and a graffito façade reworked in the 19th century, though likely according to the original model[50].

On the other side is the church of San Francesco and the adjacent convent, which together with the 16th century cloister (much restored) has been turned into a hotel. San Francesco probably dates back to the 13th century or to the first part of the 14th century and displays all of the characteristics of the sober Franciscan architecture. The façade has only one Gothic-style door, surmounted by an oculus. The interior is one open space covered by a ceiling of trusses, and the walls are covered with frescoes. Of these only a few ruined *lacerti*, discovered during the radical restorations at the turn of the century, remain on the walls. However, the frescoes of the *Stories of the Life of St. Francis* of the apse are intact, though in very bad condition. These have been attributed to Cristofano di Bindoccio and Meo di Pero, two Sienese painters of the second half of the 14th century who often worked together[51]. The frescoes on the side walls have also been attributed to them but at least a few must be the work of another hand, such as *The Mystic Marriage of St. Catherine*

Church of San Francesco, Cristofano di Bindoccio and Meo di Pero, Stories from the Life of St. Francis

and the figures of the *Saints John the Evangelist and Peter,* frescoes dating to the 1340's and attributable to the Sienese painter Niccolò di Ser Sozzo[52].

The Corso Rossellino ends at Porta al Prato. Outside the wall, one arrives in the modern **Piazza Dante Alighieri**. Above the city gate is a modern mural painted by the Pientine artist Aleardo Paolucci.

The piazza, which is set up as a public garden, houses the *Monument to the Fallen in World War I,* designed by the architect Gino Chierici and executed by the Sienese sculptor Ettore Brogi, supervised by Emilio Gallori. The monument was inaugurated in December 1923.

Coming out of the piazza and taking the main road one may go on to San Quirico d'Orcia by way of a beautiful, panoramic road.

Going the other direction on this same road one arrives in Monticchiello. In coming out of the piazza to the left two other roads lead out of piazza Dante Alighieri.

One is the road of Santa Caterina, which is a pleasant walk to the **church** of the same name. This is a brick structure dating to the end of the 17th century or perhaps to the 18th century. Inside is the grand *fresco* of the Sienese school of the 13th century, which was brought here from a roadside tabernacle and towards which the local population showed great devotion. The heads of the *Madonna and Child* are the

Villa Benocci, Dario Neri, Autumn and Winter from the Allegory of the Air

only visible parts of the fresco, as it is now covered by a 17th century canvas.

In front of the church of Santa Caterina is the attractive **Villa Benocci**, built in 1923. It was designed by the architect Gino Chierici, in a style that recalls the Viennese architecture of the turn of the century.

The interior is largely decorated by *murals depicting allegories* of the four elements and other decorative subjects, painted by the Sienese artist Dario Neri between 1924 and 1925[53].

THE ROMITORIO

Going around the back of the church and down a small alley, we arrive at the striking romitorio.

One arrives by going down a tight stairway. Halfway down one will find a small chapel, the back wall of which holds a ruined relief, perhaps of the 16th century, depicting the *Madonna del latte*. New mothers came to pray before this rare image – the Madonna's hand has six fingers. The monks were responsible for looking after the romitorio below, as before

Above and below, two images of the romitorio

they had been responsible for the fresco in the edicola which is now in the church.

Continuing down the steps one comes to the romitorio, which is completely dug out of tufa. Its origins are ancient, though there have been continuous transformations, and unfortunately the romitorio has been left to deteriorate in recent times. It is still possible to reconstruct the various spaces inhabited by the hermits.

Entering, on the left, is the chapel, which maintains very faint traces of frescoes. There are the cells and other rooms with sculptures which must have constituted a remarkable complex but which are reduced today to mere fragments that are difficult to date. Much of this must date back to the 14th or 15th century, though certain images, such as the two-tailed siren which also appears in the architrave of the pieve of San Vito, are without a doubt much older.

THE PIEVE DEI SANTI VITO AND MODESTO

One arrives by continuing the walk from Santa Caterina or, from Piazza Dante Alighieri, by walking towards Via Fonte, and from the center of town by descending the stairs from Porta al Santo, right behind the apse of the Duomo.

The Pieve di Corsignano

The pieve has been mentioned since the 13th century (though as the baptistery of San Vito in Rutiliano) and has undergone various transformations in the course of time[54]. The oldest parts of the church are the Ravenna-like cylindrical

Pieve di Corsignano, façade

tower, which was later made into a bell-tower and inserted into the façade, and the little crypt made up of small cross vaults and one single column in the center. This was probably built for use as a *sacrario* for reliquaries or as a funerary ipogeo. It is made of the local dark colored sand stone.

The façade, decorated above with suspended arches, has one double lancet window with a caryatid to substitute the column, and which seems, for all its naked nobility, to hearken back to Etruscan sculpture.

The decoration of the door and the architrave are most interesting; these are usually dated to around the 11th-12th centuries, but they seem much older. The architrave in particular does not display Christian figures or allegories, but instead shows evidence of a pagan origin. The two sirens, one of which is seen in the act of working with a hammer and chisel while a monstrous fish speaks into her ear, and the other with two tails, identical to that of the nearby romitorio, holds

Pieve di Corsignano, detail of the architrave of the door

up her finlike extremities in a gesture of offering, symbolizing fertility.

It is very likely that the entire area where the pieve and romitorio stand, inhabited surely as far back as Prehistory due to the presence of a spring, with its pleasant climate and fertile fields, had a long tradition of fertility cults, of which the devotion to the *Madonna del latte* would be merely a more "modern" version [55]. On the right side is another door, later than the first, with an architrave upon which is depicted, with a clearer sense of decoration and symmetry, the *Journey of the Magi* and the *Sacred Family* without St. Joseph, which follows Byzantine tradition. The interior is separated by square pillars into three naves, of which the right was built in the 12th century to enlarge the church, and is undecorated except for two entwined serpents carved into the capital of the last pillar of the left nave. It is here that one finds the bowl of the antique baptismal fount where Enea Silvio Piccolomini was baptized. The fount's capital and base are fragments that come from the ruined pieve di Santa Maria. Some fragments of a High Medieval (first half of the 9th century?) barrier were found during the digs of a restoration project in 1925 and can now be seen in the presbytery, to the right of the altar.

TOWARDS PORTA AL CIGLIO

If, instead of proceeding from the piazza to the right toward Porta al Prato, one walks on the other side we immediately come to the palazzi of the Cardinals. Alongside Palazzo Borgia, along the Corso Rossellino, we find that which is most likely the palazzo of the Cardinal Artebatense and this is followed by the palazzo of Niccolò Forteguerri, the palazzo of Gregorio Lolli, though some think that it is leaning against Palazzo Ammannati and finally, that of Cardinal Gonzaga[56].

To the right of the Corso are some small streets with rather romantic names: Via della Fortuna and Via dell'Amore, which go around Palazzo Gonzaga, and then Via del Bacio and Via Buia. All of these flow into Via del Casello which runs above the rest of the wall of the city.

In this way one arrives at Porta al Ciglio in which one finds other bastions of the wall into which a monastery was built. This was later transformed into a women's conservatory, the Conservatorio of San Paolo, where on the altar of the church of the same name one finds a beautiful canvas datable to 1620-1625, by the Sienese painter Francesco Rustici, called "Il Rustichino". An oil on paper sketch of this piece, which depicts the *Madonna and Child with Saints Carlo Borromeo, Francis, Clare, Catherine of Siena, and John the Baptist,* is also to be found in the same conservatory[57].

SPEDALETTO

One arrives at the walled castle of Spedaletto by taking the road which leads to the Via Cassia and which crosses the Val d'Orcia to Bagno Vignoni. Built in the 12th century to serve as a hospital, that is, as a hospice for travellers and pilgrims along the Via Francigena, near the bridge crossing the river Orcia (the ruins are still visible looking down at the river), it became the *grancia* of the Hospital of Santa Maria della Scala in Siena nearly a century later. It is a large castle with battlements and towers, and though it has been reworked it is still in good condition. Inside the walls is the small church of San Niccolò consecrated in 1462, from which the Vecchietta altarpiece in the Diocesan Museum in Pienza was taken from. On the door of the church is a travertine bas relief (now actually located in the same Museum) depicting the *Madonna and Child with Musical Angels,* a modest piece whose datability is difficult to determine (ranging between the 14th and the 15th centuries) and whose placement in a particular cultural setting is uncertain. The Late Gothic flavour that is found is not enough to place the cultural provenance outside Italy, as has been suggested [58]. Carlo II d'Angiò was among the illustrious guests at the castle in 1289, as well as Pius II who, in 1460 wanted to promulgate a bill in favour of the church of Spedaletto.

The grancia *of Spedaletto*

MONTICCHIELLO

Just outside the Porta al Prato, from Pienza, is the beginning of the beautiful road to Montichiello, an ancient Medieval borgo built on a hill overlooking a wondrous panorama.

The wall of the city lined with solid towers encloses the entire inhabited portion of the town, the center of which is the church of Saints Leonard and Christopher. It is a large 13th century church with a well-made Gothic door and an elegant rose window. The interior of the church is a single nave, transformed in the 18th century. It is decorated with frescoes of the 14th and 15th century Sienese schools which re-emerged during restoration in 1933. Other frescoes cover the walls of the apse and the inside of the façade. Among these are *The Dressing of the Knight* which recalls the work of Pietro Lorenzetti, the large late 14th century fresco with St. Cristopher, and the allegorical scenes with the *Confessions of the Soul* of the same period.

Other objects worth a glance include a 16th century wooden *Crucifix* and a wrought iron gate built by Petruccio Betti da Siena (1410). Two important pieces originally came from this church and have now been moved. One is Domenico di Niccolò "dei Cori"'s *scultura lignea* depicting *St. Leonard,* which as we have seen is now in the Diocesan Museum of Pienza. The other is an extraordinary panel with the *Madonna and Child,* the central part of a polyptic painted by Pietro Lorenzetti, also

Monticchiello, gate of access to the town

Monticchiello, façade of the church of the Saints Leonard and Christopher

in the Diocesan Museum in Pienza. The sweet Madonna, however, may shortly return to its original church.

Every July in Monticchiello sees the celebrated local manifestations of the "Teatro Povero", a theatrical representation written and acted in by the local inhabitants of the borgo[59].

THE MONASTERY OF SANT'ANNA IN CAMPRENA

The monastery, founded by the "Beato" Bernardo Tolomei and inhabited, it seems, since 1334, rises up around four kilometers from Pienza, isolated in the midst of a beautiful wooded area[60]. In the years between the 15th and 16th centuries the church and monastery were completely remodelled into the Renaissance forms that we see today.

Sant'Anna in Camprena, Giovanni Antonio Bazzi called "Il Sodoma", The Multiplication of the Bread and Fishes

Sant'Anna in Camprena, Giovanni Antonio Bazzi called "Il Sodoma", The Pietà

In 1503, two years after the completion of the work on the cloister and the refectory, Giovann'Antonio Bazzi, called "Il Sodoma" was commissioned to undertake the decoration of the refectory.

The Miracle of the Bread and Fishes is depicted on the back wall. It is divided into three parts framed by arches laid out on pilasters decorated with grotesques. Over the entry, in the center above the door, we find the *Pietà,* to the left, *St. Benedict and the Olivetans,* and to the right, *St. Anne, the Madonna and Child and two Monks.* Along the side walls just above the space where there were once wooden headboards, are two friezes of extraordinary grotesques which alternate between monochrome scenes from the life of Sant'Anna and medallions with busts of the saints. The frescoes, the first work of Sodoma in Tuscany, were finished in 1504, one year before he began the grand cycle of the *Stories of St. Benedict* at the monastery of Monte Oliveto Maggiore. They provide evidence not only of the Lombard, leonardesque origin of his work, but also of a firm adherence to the methods of Peruginesque classicism that was expanding across Central Italy[61]. All of the frescoes were detached and replaced in their positions during restorations in 1970.

In the vicinity of the monastery is the tiny borgo of **Castelmuzio**, where it is possible to visit the small parochial museum with its primarily Sienese school paintings of various periods, goldworks, and ornaments. Those wishing to go on for a few kilometers, to Montisi, will find there one of the most beautiful panels of the Sienese Quattrocento, signed by Neroccio di Bartolomeo and dated 1496.

NOTES

[1] On the birth of Pienza the indispensible sources are, obviously, the *Commentarii* by Enea Silvio Piccolomini (edited by. L. Totaro, Milan 1984); see also E. CARLI, *Pienza. La città di Pio II,* Rome 1966 and A. OLIVETTI, *Costruito instabile,* in *Conferenze d'arte,* edited by G. Mazzoni, Montepulciano 1994, pp. 17-50.

[2] A useful synopsis on this theme can be found in the little book by I. PETRI, *Storia breve di una simbolica città,* Genoa 1972.

[3] For a more in-depth study of the life of Enea Silvio Piccolomini see (besides the *Commentarii*): L. VON PASTOR, *Storia dei papi dalla fine del Medioevo,* (1894), Rome 1961; E. GARIN, *Ritratto di Enea Silvio Piccolomini,* in ID., *Ritratti di umanisti,* Florence 1967, pp. 9-39; C. NAVILLE, *Enea Silvio Piccolomini. L'uomo, l'umanista, il Pontefice (1405-1464),* Locarno 1984.

[4] The direct responsibility of Alberti in the project for Pienza has been much emphasised by J. Pieper recently, while the observance of Alberti's principles, already underlined by Carli (*Pienza* cit., p. 45), has been accentuated again in G.C. ROMBY, *Modelli urbanistici rinascimentali. La vicenda di Pienza,* in *Conferenze d'arte* cit., pp. 51-67, pp. 55-57.

[5] On the restoration work, ancient and modern, of the Cathedral see in particular: A. BARBACCI, *Il restauro del Duomo di Pienza,* in "La Diana", IX, 1934, pp. 5-134 and *Il Duomo di Pienza 1459-1984. Studi e restauri,* edited by M. Forlani Conti, Florence 1992.

[6] A page of great literary beauty on the light in the Duomo of Pienza has been written by E. CARLI, *Pienza* cit., p. 37.

[7] E. CARLI, *Pienza* cit., pp. 99-100.

[8] The epigram of Pius II is taken from E. CARLI, *Pienza* cit., p. 62, n. 21: "PARVA FUI NUPER QUALIS DELUBRA DECERET / ET NON URBANI MOENIA PRESSA LOCI / MOX PIUS UT TEMPLUM CONSTRUXIT ET INTULIT URBEM / QUANTAM URBS ATQUE AEDES POSTULAT ESSE IUBET / ERGO PIENTINOS SI LATIUS IMPLEO CAMPOS / NUNC URBI NUPER OPPIDULO SONUI A.D. MCCCCLXIII / GIHANES TOFANI DE SENIS ME FECIT".

[9] J. PIEPER, *Un ritratto di Leon Battista Alberti architetto: osservazioni su due capitoli emblematici nel Duomo di Pienza (1462),* in *Leon Battista Alberti,* edited by A. Engel and J. Rykwert, exhibition catalogue, Milan 1994, pp. 54-63.

[10] On the paintings in the Duomo cf. P. PALLADINO, "*Pittura in una casa di vetro": un riesame e una proposta sul programma decorativo di Pio II per la cattedrale di Pienza,* in "Prospettiva", n. 75-76, July-October 1994, pp. 100-108; see also E. CARLI, *Pienza* cit., and R. BARTALINI, *Il tempo di Pio II,* in *Francesco di Giorgio e il Rinascimento a Siena,* edited by L. Bellosi, exhibition catalogue, Milan 1993, pp. 92-105.

[11] E. CARLI, *Pienza* cit., p. 102.

[12] See the article by L. CAVAZZINI in *Francesco di Giorgio* cit., pp. 10-13.

[13] See for example the wooden statue of *St. Bernardino of Siena* now in the Bargello Museum in Florence and the bronze of the *Risen Christ* which hangs in the church in the Hospital of Santa Maria della Scala in Siena.

[14] See E. CARLI, *Pienza* cit., pp. 115-116, pp. 134-137, n. 49 and L. MARTINI, *Museo Diocesano di Pienza*, Siena 1998, pp. 69-70.

[15] P. TORRITI, *Pienza, la città del rinascimento italiano,* Genoa 1992, p. 17.

[16] On the Diocesan Museum and its masterpieces see L. MARTINI, *Museo Diocesano* cit.

[17] For a first approach to this argument see the article by A.M. GUIDUCCI in *Pienza e la Val d'Orcia. Opere d'arte restaurate dal XIV al XVII secolo,* Genoa 1988, pp. 10-13.

[18] On this mass book see the article by G. DAMIANI in *Restauri a Montefollonico,* edited by L. Martini, Siena 1991, pp. 19-27.

[19] On these two objects see the articles by L. MARTINI in *Panis Vivus,* edited by C. Alessi and L. Martini, exhibition catalogue, Siena 1994, pp. 94-96.

[20] E. CARLI, *Pienza* cit., pp. 54-59, n. 13.

[21] M. MEISS, *Italian Primitives at Konopiste,* in "The Art Bulletin", XXVIII, 1, March 1946, pp. 1-16.

[22] P. TORRITI, *Pienza* cit., pp. 47-50.

[23] C. BRANDI, *Reintegrazione di Bartolo di Fredi,* in "Bullettino Senese di Storia Patria", XXXVIII, 1931, pp. 206-210, now in ID., *Pittura a Siena nel Trecento,* Turin 1991, pp. 169-173.

[24] Cf. E. CARLI, *Il Sassetta e il Maestro dell'Osservanza,* Milan 1957, pp. 122-123 and L. MARTINI, *Museo Diocesano* cit., p. 38 e 44..

[25] E. CARLI, *Pienza* cit., p. 140.

[26] For the dating and attributions of the two wooden statues, see the articles by A. BAGNOLI in *Scultura dipinta. Maestri di legname e pittori a Siena 1250-1450,* exhibition catalogue, Florence 1987, pp. 119-121 and pp. 127-128.

[27] On the three tapestries see L. MARTINI, *Museo Diocesano* cit., pp. 54-61.

[28] The attribution is owed to G. CANTELLI (*Il Piviale di Pio II,* in *Conferenze d'arte* cit., pp. 69-84) and ID., *Storia dell'oreficeria e dell'arte tessile in Toscana dal Medioevo all'età moderna,* Florence 1996, pp. 40-41. This hypotesis do not convince L. MARTINI (*Museo Diocesano* cit., pp. 62-67).

[29] See the article by L. MARTINI in *Pienza e la Val d'Orcia* cit., pp. 44-48.

[30] See the article by L. MARTINI in *Pienza e la Val d'Orcia* cit., pp. 49-50.

[31] Cf. the article by M. COLLARETA in *Francesco di Giorgio* cit., pp. 148-149.

[32] Cf. the article by M. COLLARETA in *Francesco di Giorgio* cit., pp. 150-151.

[33] Cf. E. CARLI, *Pienza* cit., pp. 109-110.

[34] Cf. E. CARLI, *Pienza* cit., p. 115, p. 134 n. 48.

[35] Cf. the article by L. MARTINI in *Pienza e la Val d'Orcia* cit., pp. 54-57.

[36] Cf. M. MACCHERINI in *Francesco di Giorgio* cit., pp. 318-321.

[37] For the attribution to Signorelli (first proposed by Ragghianti) and the probable provenance of the panel in the church of Santa Maria and Lucia in Montepulciano – now in the Uffizi – see E. CARLI, *Pienza* cit., pp. 60-61, n. 16.

[38] Cf. P. TORRITI, *Pienza* cit., p. 27 and M. CIATTI, in *Pienza e la Val d'Orcia* cit., pp. 58-60 and the article by S. PADOVANI, in *L'età di Savonarola. Fra' Bartolomeo e la Scuola di San Marco,* exhibition catalogue, edited by S. Padovani, Venice 1996, pp. 83-84.

[39] The silks in the Pienza Museum are published in G. CANTELLI, *Lampassi figurati del Rinascimento nel territorio di Siena,* in *Drappi, velluti, taffettà et altre cose. Antichi tessuti a Siena e nel suo territorio,* edited by M. Ciatti, Siena 1994, pp. 60-86.

[40] Cf. L. MARTINI, *Museo Diocesano* cit., p. 108.

[41] Cf. the article by A. BAGNOLI, in *Pienza e la Val d'Orcia* cit., pp. 64-65.

[42] See the articles by A. BAGNOLI, in *Domenico Beccafumi e il suo tempo,* exhibition catalogue, Milan 1990, pp. 572-575 and in *Restauri a Montefollonico* cit., pp. 46-49.

[43] Cf. E. CARLI, *Pienza* cit., pp. 118-123.

[44] Cf. E. CARLI, *Pienza* cit., pp. 118-123 and L. MARTINI, *Museo Diocesano* cit., pp. 118-126 and 137-140.

[45] Cf. L. MARTINI, *Museo Diocesano* cit., p. 108.

[46] Cf. the article by L. MARTINI in *Panis Vivus,* edited by C. Alessi and L. Martini, exhibition catalogue, Siena 1994, p. 130.

[47] On these fabrics, see the articles in the catalogue *Drappi, velluti, taffettà* cit., pp. 112-113, 118, 143.

[48] These notes on the archaeological collection were drawn up by Alberto Dondoli to whom I express my heartfelt thanks for his competence and his kindness. For a more profound examination consult M. MONACI, *Monumenti etruschi e italici nei Musei italiani e stranieri: Catalogo del Museo Archeologico Vescovile di Pienza,* Florence 1965.

[49] See scheda by L. MARTINI in *Pienza e la Val d'Orcia* cit., pp. 51-53.

[50] For the proposal to recognise this palazzo not as belonging to the Cardinal of Arras, but to Salomone Piccolomini see A. SCHIAVO, *Monumenti di Pienza,* Milan 1942, cited by E. CARLI, *Pienza* cit., p. 30.

[51] Cfr. S. PADOVANI, *Sulla traccia di Cristoforo di Bindoccio e Meo di Pero,* in "Bollettino d'Arte", 67, 1982, pp. 85-98 and P. TORRITI, *Pienza* cit., p. 52.

[52] Cfr. S. PADOVANI, *Sulla traccia* cit., p. 88.

[53] For this cycle see M. PIERINI, *La decorazione di Villa Benocci a Pienza,* in *Dario Neri,* exhibition catalogue, Siena 1996, pp. 71-78.

[54] For the pieve see I. MORETTI, R. STOPANI, *Romanico senese,* Florence 1981 and M.G. PAOLINI, *Un edificio di origine altomedievale dell'antica diocesi aretina, in Arezzo e il suo territorio nell'Alto Medioevo,* Cortona 1985, pp. 189-235.

[55] For the symbolism in the sculptures over the two doors and their dates, we found particularly convincing the reasoning in S. BERNARDINI, *Pievi toscane. Arte e religiosità del mondo contadino,* Turin 1985.

[56] G. CATALDI, *Pienza e la sua Piazza: nuove ipotesi tipologiche di lettura,* in "Documenti di Architettura", 7, April 1978; see also P. TORRITI, *Pienza* cit., p. 35 and F. PELLEGRINI, *Pienza. Il sogno dell'umanista,* Cortona 1995, pp. 71-82.

[57] Cfr. the article by A. BAGNOLI in *Pienza e la Val d'Orcia* cit., pp. 80-81.

[58] Cfr. the article by A.M. GUIDUCCI in *Pienza e la Val d'Orcia* cit., pp. 40-41.

[59] For the "teatro povero", see M. GUIDOTTI, *Il Teatro Povero di Montichiello,* Padua 1974; for Montichiello see V. NERI, *Montichiello, storia di una comunità,* Siena 1975.

[60] For the monastery and its frescoes, cfr. E. CARLI, *Il Sodoma a Sant'Anna in Camprena,* Florence 1974.

[61] For the early activity of Sodoma see the recent reconstruction in R. BARTALINI, *Le occasioni del Sodoma. Dalla Milano di Leonardo alla Roma di Raffaello,* Rome 1996.

BIBLIOGRAPHY

A. BARBACCI, *Il restauro del Duomo di Pienza,* in "La Diana", IX, 1934, pp. 5-134

S. BERNARDINI, *Pievi toscane. Arte e religiosità del mondo contadino,* Turin, 1985.

G. CANTELLI, *Il Piviale di Pio II*, in *Conferenze d'arte*, edited by G. Mazzoni, Montepulciano 1994, pp. 69-84.

G. CANTELLI, *Storia dell'oreficeria e dell'arte tessile in Toscana dal Medioevo all'età moderna*, Florence 1996.

E. CARLI, *Pienza. La città di Pio II,* Rome 1966.

E. CARLI, *Il Sodoma a Sant'Anna in Camprena,* Florence 1974.

Il Duomo di Pienza 1459-1984. Studi e restauri, edited by M. Forlani Conti, Florence 1992.

L. FINELLI, S. ROSSI, *Pienza tra ideologia e realtà,* Bari 1979.

Francesco di Giorgio e il Rinascimento a Siena, edited by L. Bellosi, exhibition catalogue, Milan, 1993.

E. GARIN, *Ritratto di Enea Silvio Piccolomini*, in ID., *Ritratti di umanisti,* Florence 1967, pp. 9-39.

C.R. MACK, *Pienza. The Creation of a Renaissance City,* London 1987.

G.B. MANNUCCI, *Pienza arte e storia,* Pienza 1927[2].

L. MARTINI, *Museo Diocesano di Pienza*, Siena 1998.

A. OLIVETTI, *Costruito instabile,* in *Conferenze d'arte,* edited by G. Mazzoni, Montepulciano 1994, pp. 17-50.

P. PALLADINO, *"Pittura in una casa di vetro": un riesame e una proposta sul programma decorativo di Pio II per la cattedrale di Pienza*, in "Prospettiva", 75-76, July-October 1994, pp. 100-108.

Panis Vivus, edited by C. Alessi and L. Martini, exhibition catalogue, Siena 1994.

F. PELLEGRINI, *Pienza. Il sogno dell'umanista,* Cortona 1995.

F. PELLEGRINI, *Pienza. La città utopia,* Cortona.

F. PELLEGRINI, *Messaggi nel tufo. Dalla pieve di Corsignano alle pievi della Val d'Orcia,* Città di Castello.

Pienza e la Val d'Orcia. Opere d'arte restaurate dal XIV al XVII secolo, Genoa 1984.

J. PIEPER, *Un ritratto di Leon Battista Alberti architetto: osservazioni su due capitoli emblematici nel Duomo di Pienza (1462),* in *Leon Battista Alberti,* edited by A. Engel and J. Rykwert, exhibition catalogue, Milan 1994, pp. 54-63.

J. PIEPER, *Pienza. Ser Entwurf einer humanischen Weltsicht,* Stuttgart-London 1997.

Preziosità dei Papi senesi, exhibition catalogue, Siena 1996.

M. PIERINI, *La decorazione di Villa Benocci a Pienza,* in *Dario Neri*, exhibition catalogue, Siena 1996, pp. 71-78.

Restauri a Montefollonico, edited by L. Martini, Siena 1991.

G.C. ROMBY, *Modelli urbanistici rinascimentali. La vicenda di Pienza,* in *Conferenze d'arte,* edited by G. Mazzoni, Montepulciano 1994, pp. 51-67.

A. TÖNNESMANN, *Pienza. Städtebau und Humanismus Hirmer,* München 1990.

P. TORRITI, *Pienza, la città del rinascimento italiano,* Genoa 1992[5].

Index of artists